Hello

It plays

Over and over in my mind from time to time
Thoughts constantly forward to capacity and then rewind
At times, I find myself blind to signs of different kinds
Faith rely on the meaning that's defined from the query applied

Inside I try to strive to confide in his divine words faithfully
Prophecies lead by the Trinity that can foresee the tread of my destiny
Ends the devastation that let the frustration get the best of me
Healing with the trials of victory from the dealings of my past history

How can I believe in a Superior Being of Kings that I've never seen?
He revealed to me things that I needed to see or it comes to me in my dreams
I couldn't defeat emotions that run deep so intense and steep it sinks
Until my beliefs started to convince me, that was how I use to think

I've learned to never question his will, just live til the emotions set still
It was hard for me to deal with the agony and ills of an eternal ordeal
On 1/8 was the judgment date of fate that made way for a soul to partake
But you pulled us through the years we wept until his last breath was left

The mode captured the raptures that hold my condition of remission
Intentions to implore the hopes that restored my visions of redemption
When he spoke to me, I walked with thee and my inner peace increased
Write my wrong and he forgave for all my mistakes and made it complete

Written by
Cheryl Campbell-Divinity

Prayer worked for me!

I AM

A butterfly defined by the passion that resides inside of me
Colors of nature is out lined with the earth's tones and free of impurities
A quest to seek the identity of me spiritually for peace and serenity
Believe and you will see that integrity holds the key to prosperity

A dreamer true believer that a clever plot endeavor is well conceived
A vision that's foreseen is formed through an image of a possible dream
Views are seen through the predictions of seers' visible means
Having a keen perception of an advancement of what the future reads

A teacher but before a scholar, the skills I've learned have earned me honors
The opportunities that enhanced my chances to advance in future plans ponders
Passion for deep desires to climb higher was inspired by my mentor
The knowledge that's gained has remained and what's obtained is passed to my
successor

A poetess writer of poetry, subjects combined with rhythm defines creativity
An utterance of words spoken in a metaphorical lingo formality
Lyrics written that contain emotions and sensibilities enact to capacity
The text that has needed to reach peak comes to mind naturally

A woman phenomenal brought up to become my own dependable individual
Sentimental use of traditional values descend from a wise muse who know true
potential
Exposed intensely with a gift that was given to me of femininity so sensual
A trend was made, raised self-worth praised -the grand show all the woman that I
am

Written by
Cheryl Campbell-Divinity

I can be any woman

I want to be!!

My Next Life

In my next life, I want to be
A strong educated black man with a college degree
Still yearning for higher learning while earning my P.H. D
Well- educated mind elevated now escalated to a Doctorate
Decree

I'll choose my wife carefully to spend my life and start a family
Set her on a throne that seats right next to me
Treat her like the queen that she deserves to be
Place her on a pedestal that will never fall most of all respectfully

The kids that we raise will be cherished and praised
Love is unconditional and accepted of all additional ways
There will be days filled with unpredictable rain and haze
To make it in life you have to live it right and abide by, it pays

From views and intuitions from my previous life ambitions
It's my true intention to complete the mission I was given
As I envision a rendition and guide it through with wisdom
A new world creation is built from the foundation has risen

Written by
Cheryl Campbell-Divinity

Cat in the Black Hat

One day, I was running late on my way to compete at a poetry meet
While practicing my piece, a black car stopped in front of me
After a short brief, the door had open from the back seat
Then a pair of feet of royal blue gators had stepped out onto the concrete

Then after, out come a man tall in stature that was well dressed and quite dapper
He started with his apologies for blocking the way to my destiny
Extended his hand and I did the same, he kissed the tip and we exchange names
He explained when he descend his windowpane his hat blew into the breeze

No, I replied, my mind was on the time, your hat I have not seen
However, I did see something bleak that flew passed me and blew down the street
He quickly intervened and digressed with another subject and confessed
Never again, he mentioned that black hat because he had other intentions

He had invited me that evening to spend quiet time to do whatever comes to mind
I did find me being enticed by his line, as he insist, I had to resist at this time
After seeing a gleam beaming from his gold teeth, I had to decline
No more delay and nothing more to say, I did proceed on my way to recite my
rhymes

Written by
Cheryl Campbell-Divinity

No Apologies

I wish that people could see what I believe
Learned to put my trust in God first and then me
For those who intervene and try to impede my victory
I will proceed and keep fulfilling my needs with no apologies

It took years of getting over my fears of expression to my peers
Concerned with jeers, mocks and sneers that may appear
Clear to see from mere to severe images adhered
Allowing others to stifle my new life cycle to premier

Changes been made completely starting with the acceptance of me
My self-doubt decreased when I started thinking differently
Lengths of validity commence until I reach the end of my destiny
I am going to keep doing me with no apologies

Written by
Cheryl Campbell-Divinity

8

Diva

Attention started commencing when she stepped out on the scene
Could see people staring and hear voice whispering
Still pondering while wondering who could she be
She looks so familiar to me, where could she been seen

Taken by her fascination of seduction and admiration
Adulation enhances her esteem advancement and elation
The way her motions sway don't take much persuade
Amazed of her sophisticated traits that display her deity ways

She comes with attitude not with an attitude
Always includes her crew in all of her rendezvous
With her sultry talk and the seductive way she walks and moves
She could rule the whole grove if that's what she chooses to do

Complete her best to impress with loveliness and elegance
Many express their interest to confess the classiness of the temptress
Confidence permits to her commit to success and independence
Her mission is unlimited with the conveniences to expose her image

Written by
Cheryl Campbell-Divinity

Circle of Diva's

Cheryl & Karen

Anissa, Cheryl & Mama

There is a Diva in every woman!!!

Darker Side of Me

A little girl got lost on her way to blissful days of serenity
But found by a stranger with malicious thoughts of danger and lewd tendencies
That stole her virginity before she had reach puberty
Intentionally prey on her physically instantly affected her mentally

The years passed on, her frustration have grown, more anger is shown
Her heart grew cold as stone; being afraid and alone, hope is too far-gone to move on
With depression remained from stress and strain she became emotionally drained
She sees life differently; misery is her only company where her energy is drawn

Dismay continues to invade and made way through with no escape
In a delusional state, she envisioned the face in her portrait fade away
In denial most days, her actions spoke in other ways of confession
Hostility, pain, and aggression showed on her facial expression

I keep having visions and dreams of me down on my knees
Asking the lord to forgive me for what he about to see
Take a permanent sleep on a co-dependency to delete the painful memories
But is there still a place in heaven for me to be so my mind can finally be free

Then faith was sent to me to mend and I repent from my vigorous sins
A new beginning that starts from within, is where my healing begins
Therefore, I ran through the burning sand with no weapon formed in hand
To carry on with what God planned for where this fallen angel to land

Written by
Cheryl Campbell-Divinity

Weekend

Monday is the first day of dismay, can't wait to get away
Around Tuesday noon bound is when I start my count down
On my way right up to hump day, hoping to get past Thursday
When the deadlines meet and your work load is complete
Then you have reached the end of the week

Can't concentrate with thoughts to engage in an array of escapades
It pays to get away and escape for the next two days
Plans are in effect to request a romantic conquest to connect
Make gestures of pleasures to lovers or significant others to affect

You can feel free to flee with a spree of social activities
Spend it quietly sipping on green with a good book to read
Relax to a smooth jazz tune that grooves and soothes with a mellow
beat
Or catch up on your sleep to get a fresh start for the next week

Make amends within to suspend any though s of work to blend that
comes in
Then begin with your friends to start a weekly trend to attend
Indulge and binge in a plan during the extended weekends
When it all comes to an end, then next weekend do it all over again

Written by
Cheryl Campbell-Divinity

A Letter to My Son

I still imagine just years ago
When I've witnessed a divine miracle
You were only minutes old when I held you close to my soul
I had never felt a love that is so unconditional

As the years went my heart, permit me to submit even more bliss
Since that blessed event I still hold on to your amazement
We will proceed to protect the dreams that I will forever hold
I had high hopes even before my water had broke

I will never forsake or take away your faith
Find the strength to resist and what it takes to face the world of negate
Keep strong and hold on because I will never leave you alone
Determination and desire will inspire you to aim higher

I understand that I can't teach you how to be a man
I can advise and plan to put it all in God's hands
You have the ability to reach and exceed through life's expectancies
Believe that you can stand and be the man that you need to be

Written by
Cheryl Campbell-Divinity

Cheryl & son David

P.S.

Recently you seem to believe that it take faith to move on
Now that you are grown with a son of your own
Teach him to grow and become a man that's strong
With all the conditions and discipline that you were shown

Don't stop at your son, each one, teach one, mentoring is never done
All that you do, he is looking up to you and watching your every move
Whatever you do, never let your anger and emotions consume you
Negative influences can affect his endurance if continued, him you will lose

Your positive endeavors can have an impact that will never sever
Time spent together is valued and treasured that can affect him beyond
measures
It takes a strong figure to lead and proceed with guidance and love to exceed
To my son, I will always keep this letter embedded in my heart forever

Love You Always,

In a Childs Eyes

In a Childs eyes is where the angels hide
To provide sight and guide through the beginning of life
Despise or hold pride until you reveal to them another side
Grace strengthened the faith that awaits and lies inside a child's eyes

Seeking the lure of a mentor or a prominent figure to endure
Who can adhere a future with the insure to be secure
But at the same time searching with those same eyes
The source of choice that they fine can incline to their demise

A child's eyes can assume that everything's viewed is brand new
Their sight can hold all what that they are exposed to
Insistence bring intense tendencies to an existing scene
Fields of visions and images compiled in the eyes of a child

Seek until they reach the extremities to their destiny
The need to proceed with the intervene of a higher being
Pray for a way to escape through a twist of faith from disarray
In time the truth will reveal and arise inside of a child's eyes

Written by
Cheryl Campbell-Divinity

David and son Jay'den

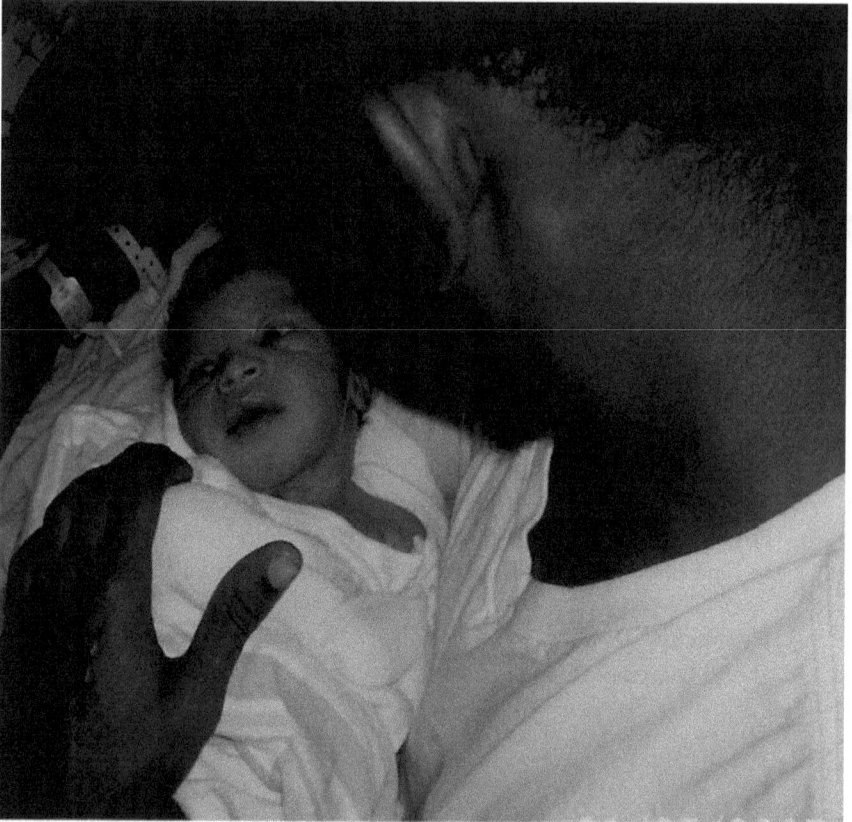

Fathers make the best mentors!!

Mind Drift

Many times, I try to find a single thought in mind
Until another decides to sneak, up from behind and intertwine
Pry and scheme into my dreams of creativity and pushed it behind
Combined vision of vivid images submitted in shift sometimes my mind just drift

My mind does choose to cruise down different avenues
And loses the original thought that was in use
It usually intrude inside a room that it don't pertain too
In addition, refuses to continue to elude the actual subject in view

Other stimulation found ways to break my concentration
Mind racing distracts channels of vast sudden acts of flash backs
Memories attack and reenact the past that holds a mass impact
Trying to cope with staying focus is sometimes hopeless

When my conscience mind has awakened, it conquers and over taken
The thoughts are now breaking away and dissipation by fading
Concentration with peace and meditation keep it from escaping
Wondering can I lift my attention span and expand my mind drifting again

Written by
Cheryl Campbell-Divinity

Issues- part 1

I've been married to the same man for seven years
He was so good to me beloved, devoted, and sincere
Besides him being a good provider, we seem happy it appears
But deep inside of me, if you can closely, you'd see the tears

Two years ago it changed; things haven't been the same since
Friends tried to tell me it will get better, but I wasn't' convinced
He ignored me constantly; didn't speak, just passed right by me
Stop spending time with the family and started running the streets

I yearned for his touches with so much desire and need
I'd beg and plead for his affection but he refused to be near me
It would repeat nightly, I'd cry myself to sleep silently
So I discovered another lover who satisfied me so completely

Now regretting ever letting this start and taking it this far
Being scorned has torn us apart when he disregarded my heart
Should I tell him what I did knowing that he couldn't handle it?
How could I break it to him that our youngest kid might not be his?

Written by
Cheryl Campbell-Divinity

Issues-part 2

We had so much to discuss beginning with the matters of trust
This included the issues that concern the both of us
His eyes filled with tears when I revealed that the baby was not his
But it appeared I wasn't alone he has secrets of his own he hid

He had confessed to me the reason why he hadn't fulfill my needs
As he proceed to tell me there is someone else he sees
I sunk to my knees from what he had intensely admitted to me
Stunned completely as he stated clearly that his lover is in fact is a
he

Stayed devoted to his kids even the one that isn't his
They shouldn't have to suffer from what we did
Plans for cohabitation arose with his alternative relation
After we made changes in our living arrangement situation

Anguish evolved from the pain we had caused and induced
There is no excuse to justify why we decided to hide the truth
When we saw the need to be discreet, that's when our problems grew
As long as we continue, we will always have issues

Written by
Cheryl Campbell- Divinity

Angel

You must have fallen from heaven
And landed into my world
Since the day, you come alone
My happiness has unfurled

You must be an angel
Regarding the existence of your luster
Captured my heart with your ardent touch
Set fire to my soul like no other

I will make a path through the rainbow
That leads to where true faith reveals
Unveil my devotion in your honor
The togetherness that we manifest will appear

You are my angel
That I prayed for the day that you appear
A splendid creation of greatness
A true blessing in disguise and sincere

Written by
Cheryl Campbell-Divinity

Angel of Amour!!!

Joy

You bring me joy
And lots of happiness each day
The joy of you is in every thought
Each night as I lay

The worthiness of your heart
Melts my soul with fire
The tenderness of your touch
Warms me with desire

I get so excited
With just a smell of your perfume
It sends chills up my spine
With desires in volumes

The joy that I feel
It is an everlasting love
Which I pray that it will stay
To the heavens from up above

The words that I express to you
Will never attract another decoy
My heart is true to you
Because you bring me, joy

Written by
Cheryl Campbell-Divinity

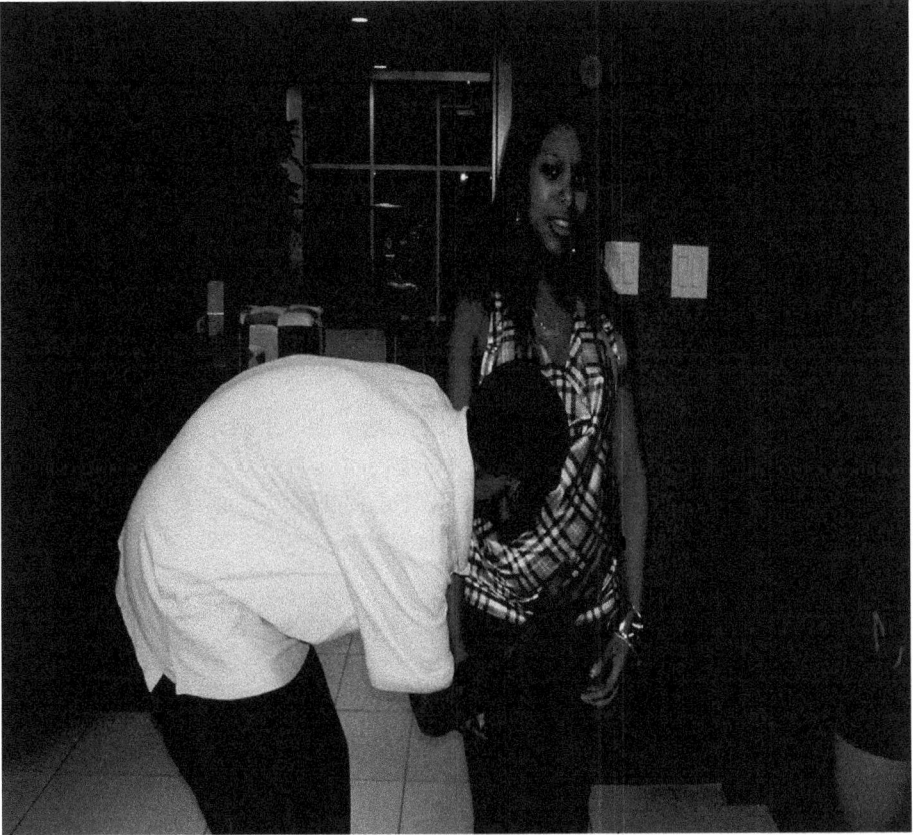

David & Zarinah

SO FULL OF JOY

Anticipation

Looking forward to ecstasy
So I'm anxiously waiting
For a chance for romance
That got me anticipating

Let's make a date to escape
For a night of amour
Full of love and affection
A night that I long for

The thought s of you next to me
Makes me shiver inside
Exploring every inch of your body
Your command I will abide

Take my hand and let me lead you
To a place for us to delegate
That explodes with ecstasy
And our destiny waits

Cherish each moment spent with you
By attending to you sensually
Aroused by your adoring sensation
Let us anticipate this moment eternally

Written by
Cheryl Campbell-Divinity

Thank You

For making and waking me up each day
And enabling me to make it out of bed with no delay
Giving me the courage to follow the path, I made
I can't predict the future so that's why I pray

Most things in my life, I have taken for granted
Like giving me sight to see to read, handed to my advantage
The senses I received help me manage to handle it
At times, I dismiss the gifts and tend to abandon the wits

I remember days when life put me down in many ways
 A lack of faith had took the place of what is intended for me to be
But I rode the guided wings of the highest superior being
Now in my noble heart I do believe that I can achieve

For lifting me and giving me the opportunity to try
I know I am a child of your that you won't deny
This life has a purpose for me to show my ability to shine
 I want to thank you for my able body, soul, and mind

Written by
Cheryl Campbell-Divinity

Pass Me By

Every day I watched, you walk toward me
Hope to capture the gloss that sparkles in your eyes
But when you see me on the streets, you don't speak
You just pass me by

A glimpse of you is worth a million stares, nothing, or all
Many times, I perceived your alluring aroma that lingers on
Watching you walk away each day until your appearance is gone
I wanted to stop you and pursue by revealing my feelings for so long

Can I persuade you to stay so I can relay to you what I need to say?
I've tried to search for someone to adore plus more I prayed each day
That love calls and it won't fade away and leave me astray
So please let me hold you on your way for just a slight delay

A chance to show you where this potential affair can lead
I guarantee that hope is the key that is a part of me I won't deny
Don't let this moment slip through I'm asking you to give it a try
There won't be an opportunity if you keep passing me by

Written by
Cheryl Campbell-Divinity

Bless the Child

Penalties applied to those that don't abide to limits and guide lines
Reality is revealed to shield eyes that hide the blindside of man kind
Early signs of prime to decline a disobedient state of mind
Discipline and guidance will yield the defiance that provoke violence

They say it takes a whole village just to raise one
Imagine what can be done if we start teaching them young
Educate a kingdom of natural born leaders about where they came from
And become the future generation of prominent icons

The world can get cold like when the wind blows and unloads frustration
Can't always take and embrace them from facing influenced temptations
The uneducated can be manipulated with the right persuasion
Idle hands will partake in the devils plans through desperation

Abiding your time will provide an inspired mind to incline
Keep reaching for the sky by climbing high up the mountainside
Mentors envision bringing out the inhibition that's instilled with wisdom
Giving them a reason to make decision on being productive citizens

Written by
Cheryl Campbell-Divinity

Terrance & Terrell

Angela & Greg

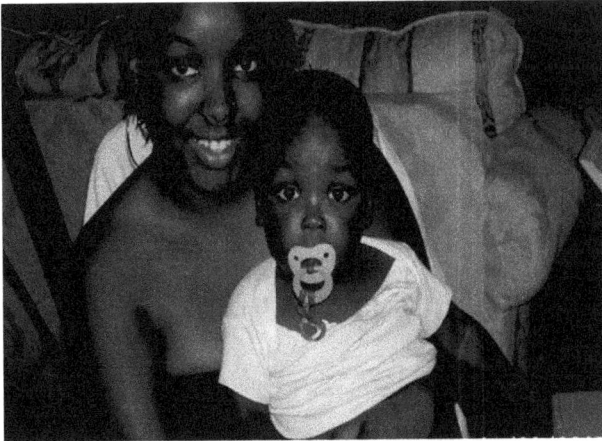

Children are a blessing!

Just Like Her

I could see that he really loved me
Young and free, around in our late teens and he respected my virginity
From our first date, we anticipate to consummate on the day we're engaged
Regret that I let my first mate get away and now it's too late to recon ciliate

Tried to dictate, control and manipulate; it didn't make him want to stay
A part of me have been this way since I was old enough to date
When the tables turned on fate, I couldn't take the aches of the heartbreaks
How many kisses does it take to fill that void, to sake that first mistake

She had always mentioned that I should be receiving more than he was giving
I developed a concept as I listened to her bitching about how much I was missing
Remembering back then seeing how she had handled different men for their ends
I started playing them like she did for money, gifts, trips, and a Benz

From the start I shouldn't have taken part and followed my own heart
Disregarded his feelings for my own selfish reasons that set us apart
Settled for less when I sold my soul to impress for meaningless assets
Honesty occurred to me and opened my eyes to see that I was being just like her

Written by
Cheryl Campbell-Divinity

Ups & Downs

Seeing, is believing that you can achieve with the ability to make it a reality
I imagined what can be if I just trust and believe and be free of insecurities
Heed to the ministries and proclaim my dignity that precedes the negativity
With the agility to build and keep the pride inside of me and pray for my enemies

The opposite of a smile is a frown turned upside
Since your problems come around, now you're scared to let your guard down
Cast of fears is conceived to believe that you're unworthy of his mercies
Questions of doubt trying to figure out a way to make it some how

I was sore before and couldn't admit that my bliss wasn't always like this
Forgive and insist that I combated for happiness, which took years of practice
With a dire need of a higher being, that can inspire me to be free
Proceed on my knees, as I plead for inner peace so it can one day reach me

Formulate a plan that came with arrangements to make changes
Deeply in my time of need, I called my mama to pray for me
Now I can clearly see and take lead toward the means to succeed
A path is paved to make a way for me to leave for others to proceed and take
lead

Written by
Cheryl Campbell-Divinity

Birth of a Buttafly

As I opened my eyes to rise to a brand new sunshine
I felt the rejoice to an uplifting voice, a given permission
To bring a song that sings in my heart like a symphony's rendition
For now I fit the descript of a woman on a mission

While sitting and wishing for a chance of a new beginning
Sacrifice my life with a plight to fight my inhibitions
By sticking to my decisions by making a commitment
Envision my ambitions and put them into existence

As I plead on bent knees the answers had come to me
It begin when a friend indeed had given me a book to read
In need of a remedy I listened to an inspirational peace on a CD
With his graces thrust upon me, my life had changed suddenly

With God as my witness I've permit the will of forgiveness
To forgive but not forget he insist I commit to contentment
He's been so good to me he enabled me to see my own eminence
He uplift me with a gift, now it's up to me to seek my riches

Defeat and buried the burdens I have carried until it perished
Demanded a chance to wear and cherish the merits I inherit
Enriched in status but still old fashion like a southern Baptist
Practice being active with diligence and magnificent tactics

Written by
Cheryl Campbell-Divinity

Buttafly symbolizes change!!!

10/10/65

He had meant more than the world to me
Seemed that we had related differently than our other siblings
Appealed naturally to others with his pleasing personality
Heart filled with love deeply but he kept fleeing to seek extreme activities

Used to verbal abuse and was ridiculed throughout his youth
Reduced his self-worth completely from the ones that he looked up to
Negated statements were embedded set in and he was confused
Compared to a disparaged individual that he never knew and yet it affected
through

As the years increased, he was beginning to believe what he had perceived
He proceeded to keep company that would commonly feed into negativity
Disbelief of his capacities did lead to his own insecurities
Got caught up in the streets with people he did meet with even more misery

One day a transition was made when we laid him in his final resting place
This was the day that mama dreaded and prayed that she didn't have to face
Now she can rest easily through the night peacefully since she know where he lays
The Lord did foresee his life through before he was given birth too
On the night that he first arrived on 10/10/65

Written by
Cheryl Campbell-Divinity

A Second Chance-pt. 1

As he laid his hands on my breast trying to revise me by pressing on my chest
I can see my life flashing from my reaction while lying here in distress
Sinking to her knees mama screaming Lord, please don't take her yet
From the severe injury, I can't seem to breathe wondering if the flat line is next

As my outer being has risen above the scene, I can see people hovered over me
Pumping for my heart to beat, mama said a prayer hoping that I'm not deceased
While my children watched me lying unconsciously on the love seat
Love illusions results to concussions and contusions now it's my life I'm losing

In a conscious dream I've heard a serene voice speak to me
It wanted to review my life for the last five years of grief
I thought about when I first lost my self-respect and dignity
The more memories increased, the more the tears ran down my cheeks

Deprived since that first cry, I tried to hide with denies and other lies
Many black eyes and bruises with excuses on how it was applied
Feed on my insecurities my useless energy had me writing my own eulogy
Needing my life redeemed, is it too late for me, or will I finally rest in peace

To end the abuse and defuse the triggered anger that kept me in danger
I looked to my savior and found a way to escape from outrageous behavior
For a chance to leave I took a good look and realize it was deep inside of me
There wasn't much that they could do left, but suddenly I started to gasp for breath

Written by
Cheryl Campbell-Divinity

A Second Chance pt. 2
The Verdict

As I was called to the witness stand sworn to truth by raising my right hand
I had to look into his mother's eyes to explain why her son is now deceased
Nervously twitching in my seat while answering questions asked repeatedly
Instantly remembering days clearly how he severely beat me

After building a case he became missing for a few days without a trace
A chance to escape I moved out of the house and into my own place
With laws of just he couldn't come near us within a 50-feet radius
He will be detain and charges will remain from violating my complaint

Somehow he had found me, then quickly assaulted me until I fell to my feet
I pulled out my peace that I kept underneath the bottom of my fake tree
He didn't stop so I cocked the rod then shot him until he dropped
I was still in shock when they came to take me away into custody

Trying to convince the court of my innocence by pleading self-defense
After the recess break the jury started to deliberate then back and forth I paced
After the judge resided, she had ordered me to rise and face the jury
I was intrigued when the foreman began to read the verdict slowly of NOT
GUILTY

Written by
Cheryl Campbell-Divinity

Mr. Saxophone Player

Pleasing from what I've seen you make it seem like it came so easily
A question is given on how the rhythm is tamed, or will it remain a mystery
Like an angel earned its wings, composed a melody on a harp string
You bring inspired felicity that makes the harmony sings to me

Enticed by the magic of your seduction during each session on percussion
Passion is set and captured the effect of desire and erects into combustion
The smooth sounds of the groove that soothes and proves that I can't resist
The gallant talent that which enhances the gifts that you were blessed with

It takes my mind away and escapes into the stories that you narrate
A spiritual stimulation generates from a sensation of energy that you create
Elated when you play and remain sweet like homemade lemonade
Appease with great ease and proceed with the peace that moves me

A sketch of your silhouette is glowing where the lit moon is set
Timeless amazement has confessed for his greatness at its best
Built a soulful rapport to store what most would adore
When your high noted sore, it make me yearn for more of your encore

Written by
Cheryl Campbell-Divinity

Mr. Mann!!

Episodes

Sometimes we see things on the outside and not looking in
Some will judge if they don't understand to begin
Others do keep silent without the violence and hold it with in
We need to teach our children the adversity can lead to sin

Some try to preach to us scriptures from the good book
Recite verses in their own versions so the passage is over looked
Mislead the congregation by sealing a deal when hands had shook
Sold for success in life, paid the highest price now your soul is took

Beauty represents a glorious nature that pleases the mind
Inner beauty is uniquely defined which most can't recognized
A portrait reveals a smile that's divine but hides what's really inside
Distress and unhappiness subside in view of the public's eyes

Years ago, you thought that you were so invincible and time would last
Live life on the fast track and now there is no turning back to undo the task
Served life severely for eternity from a serious effect that was cast
Living in denial soon the truth will come to trial and unveil the past

Written by
Cheryl Campbell-Divinity

Beauty Is

A distinctive expression of inner though
That embraces the mind's essence
Intellectually well-spoken gracefully
Applied knowledge broadens with intelligence

Heavenly features are a dominant trait
Commonly inherited from a great descendent
Revealing generations of pure loveliness
Uniqueness shows the structure to be splendid

A gift of life that is a product of love
A joyous occasion that is shared between us two
The celebration of birth is a value worth treasures
Precious moments given bring worthiness to you

A flower blossoms in the spring, moistened from the rain
Sprouting from the ground, bathing in the sun rays
A warm afternoon breeze causes the pedals to sway
Planted in the garden to grow, then picked each spring day

Written by
Cheryl Campbell-Divinity

Beautiful Things!

True

The words that I say
To you are very true
Coming from my heart
Piercing my soul through and through

You mean so much to me
Sometimes it hurts me so
Cause I'm so afraid of losing you
I don't want to let you go

You are my heart my soul my everything
My world revolves around you
You're more amazed than words that I put into a phrase
Because my heart is true

I wish that I could walk through your mind
And grant your fondest wish
Make you a true believer of me
And fulfill your dreams with bliss

Please let me back into your world
I will promise to stay true
You will not regret your decision
Because my love for you is true

Written by
Cheryl Campbell-Divinity

Drifting Heart

Sometimes I sit back and wonder
Where does my lone heart belong?
About time I come with an answer
The eager thought is long gone

I don't actually live here
I just visit from time to time
Until another calls out for me
I have to flee to be free; at least let my heart decides

I can't stay in one place for very long
Because of all my heartache and pain
Never again will I let another mold me
For all the hurtful feelings and the tears that once
rained

When I drift away from place to place
Having anguished memories that won't erase
The thoughts of settling down my heart evades
Take one day at a time to mend the broken trace

Written by
Cheryl Campbell-Divinity

An unsettled Heart will always drift away!!!!!

Music

Music is a remedy that's intended to ease and soothe the mind
The soft sounds of the melody is designed to help you to relax and unwind
With the rhythm intertwined and smooth lyrics behind the groove you will find
To be pleasingly divine now listen to them all combined and feel it deep inside

Let it take you away to another place where you were destine to be
Escape with the sensuality of the harmony that brings back memories
Oldies with the songs that brought out the Love Jones that set your heart free
A mellow jazz tune that put you in the mood for some everlasting ecstasy

An up tempo beat that would move your feet out on the dance floor
As the trembling of the bass that would have your heart racing soars
The vibrancy of the tone that shakes your bones right down to the core
Energy is flowing, sweat is pouring, but your body cries out for more

Music has a secret bond that has begun to heal your soul
The vibe in your voice when you harmonize that holds the highest note
The creativity of a symphony is conducted and notably composed
A gift to uplift your spirits with the words of gospel from a holy mode

Written by
Cheryl Campbell-Divinity

Music heals the soul!

My Gift to You

I'll send to you my heart and soul
Wrapped in love that's true
Sealed with emotions and desires
This is my gift to you

I'll make a wish upon a star
That shines like your elaborate smile
To let us come together as one
And share out sacred vows

We'll raise a unique descendent
An essential creation of two
Who will grow strong to stand-alone
This is my gift to you

Promises to honor and lover one another
Relish each moment spent together
Needing each other constantly
Let this feeling last forever

Not a day goes by that I don't realize
What this extreme life has come to
Time has shown that we have grown
That's my gift to you

Written by
Cheryl Campbell-Divinity

Love is the greatest gift

# of all!!

The adventures of love is not reaching the destination, it's the journey!!

Look Into My Eyes

Look into my eyes and tell me what you see
Use of an addictive substance that's consumed in our community
Walking the streets trying to trade sexual activity for currency
A young deprived mother trying to escape poverty

Traces of tears that had shed through the years
Reflections of emotional issues that have sadden me
Scars won't hide from the domestic violence and kept in silence
A young child scorns because of the loss of her virginity

If you **look into my eyes**, you can see the fear
Not of man but of God when the raptures are hear
I try to hold on to the hearts of my peers
Teach to my young the strife of life with terms that's endear

Many sights to see but if you blink you'll miss a session
Knowledge in power of the mind in time you'll learn life's lessons
With doses of drug injections and lack of self-protection
I'm losing my brothers and sisters to a viral infection

Look into my eyes and you will see hope at ease
And promises of our future generation to carry on the dreams
I give to you the knowledge that relies inside of me
And share with you what my wondering **eyes can see**

Written by
Cheryl Campbell-Divinity

Unconditional

All my life I've admired you
Took you into my heart, flaws and all
Accepted you generally of all your declaring ways
The love that we shared was unconditional

Thinking back on the times in our lives
When life's woe took the place of our faith
You had lifted me up to face all sorrows
And taught me to overcome with God's grace

Bridges are built and crossed over and lead through
A path where your elicit amazement will never cease
A fatigue hand was dealt to you for eternity
All challenges were over-powered, conquered and defeat

Our unity did bond and kept us as one
We conformed to confide in each another
Promises to always keep you in my heart
You were the rock that I was proud to call my brother

Written by
Cheryl Campbell-Divinity

Stranger

I've been seeing you for a while now
You're in and out of my life constantly
Sometimes you appear in thoughts of daydreams
You seem so real to me you're just a fantasy

When I close my eyes there you are again
Just standing there or lying next to me
Touching me, caressing and soothing my every need
Stroking my body gently or watching me as I sleep

When I opened my eyes, the sight of you disappears
Left me wondering who this reoccurring stranger is
Who comes and stimulate my most imaginable dreams
And can sense the desires in me by arousing the scene

Don't awake me now I don't want to face the morning breeze
Just let me lay here and grasp the climax that I've relieved
From thinking of you and the mystery that you bring
Let us do this again soon; I will meet you in my next dream

Written by
Cheryl Campbell-Divinity

De JA Vu

From birth until you leave this earth you will experience a familiar place
Somewhere you've never seen before, but been there in another age
A visit from the past was suspended in time and left out in haste
Illusions existing in a sense to illuminate, but can't convey or trace

A life-time ago it seemed I was an African Queen, ruler of all kingdoms
My subjects were loyal indeed; I stood by my king as we fought for freedom
An Egyptian goddess mother of wisdom with a supreme capability to lead
A fearless lioness roaming the jungle terrain remained wild and free

Does it all mean that I should take heed of the visions that I've seen
Act upon the ability of me to be what was interpreted in my dreams
An aura of energy burning thoroughly and intensely through me
Measures of extreme pleasures of an entity that had existence in another
century

When your life passes on, somewhere a child is born to inherit your soul
Some spirits linger on until another host comes alone to hold
And reincarnated into a delicate rebirth conceived, a breed that's ages old
Reborn again, redeemed of all past sins and changes to begin a new goal

Written by
Cheryl Campbell-Divinity

The power of women!!!

Silence So Loud

As I lie awake at night and listen
To the raindrops tap my window pain
Wishing that there were someone lying next to me
To hold and chase my loneliness away

Living under a dark and somber cloud
That hovers over my empty world
That spreads no sunshine over me
No one to comfort me, no one to referral

Existence of solitude is profound inside
Fatal thoughts of life in recluse
Creating a fortress that surrounds me
Piercing a shattered heart that has been broken in two

Moments of silence clutched my soul
Seeping through barriers as it penetrates
Longing for the touch of another heart
Dismay dictates the outcome of my fate

Written by
Cheryl Campbell-Divinity

Face Your Fears

Times in our lives when we sacrifice, it weighs you down
Wishing for the opportunity to fulfill your dreams to comes around
Waiting patiently for your destiny to finally hit ground
The chances are here then fear appears out of no-where it's been found

You've been hiding years of drear, but it shows through your tears
Love does not come with blows; it only controls to hold you near
No shield can protect your cries or hide the sorrow in your eyes
Find the strength to escape before it's too late, just face your fears

Yesterday you displayed dismay and today even more gray
Uncertainties of your future need lead to act of anxiety attacks
Distress only express unhappiness and discouragement to enact
Fear is what you confide in unless you find guidance and retry again

The situations we face from day to day remain the same
There is no one else to blame because we're afraid to make a change
Fear that's sustained came from the doubts that we've maintained
But we constantly complain instead of taking action to cure the pain

Written by
Cheryl Campbell-Divinity

Reality

Visions of the world's where you imagination escapes
To a place that was made to live out your fantasy
A depiction of how your current life was meant
An image of hidden desires that reflect on reality

Pictures of illusions painted in vivid colors visually
Ironically sketched into a delusional thought
Mind set and focuses on stability and tranquility
In reality peace and serenity is sought

A bed of roses is made and ready to be laid in
Pedals poured into a blissful shower
Moments flourish with rains of ecstasy
A reality sets in and realizes it is just a flower

Other worlds are made of picket fences and green trees
Gardens full of flowers that fully blossoms in May
Free of bias actions and mental satisfaction
But in this world we hope to make it to make it to another
day

Think things first, it could always get worst
There's someone deprived of life basic luxuries
Always someone who would love to walk in your shoes
Who pray for a better way but still they have to face reality

Written by
Cheryl Campbell-Divinity

Beautiful One

Each day I think of you endlessly
Not a moment passes by that you are on my mind
Wishing how I could talk to you exclusively
To express my feelings until the end of time

The way that you move it flows like poetry
It's the art of your seduction that captured my eye
The drops of flames that falls from your notable frame
Which contains your sultry of elegance does comply

A delicate sensation moved through me extremely
When your alluring existence pierced my soul
Longing to touch your worthiness intensely
I call out your name in silence my feelings I withhold

I'll write a song for you my beautiful one
Ballads contain the sensuality of your melody
Composed by the enticement that you give to me
It's your divine lyrics that controls my destiny

Written by
Cheryl Campbell-Divinity

Walking in the Rain-pg.1

Standing here in the rain
And reminiscing on the times
As the memories occurs
In the back of my mind

We use to play out in the rain
Like little kids in the park
Running and laughing in the day
And a quiet storm after dark

As I walk down the street
I see a couple reminding
Me of the fun we use to have
It keeps me thinking and smiling

You would meet and greet with a rose
A warm hug and a kiss
A passionate soul, a gentle touch
It's those rainy days what I miss

Walking hand in hand
You serenade as we stand
Lovey-dovey side by side
Creating rain storms, as

Walking in the Rain-pg.2

We shared this special one
Between a girl and a boy
While the rain drops hit my face
To hide my tears of joy

The feelings took control
Lead to a warm embrace
With a desire pitch
Followed by a smile in my face

It came to my surprise
The amour we kept inside
Bond together to last forever
On the wings of paradise

The memories came in clear
Like the storms up above
Cause I was walking in the rain
With the one I love

Written by
Cheryl Campbell-Divinity

Two became as one
When we huddled close together
Holding each other close
As we shared an umbrella

Don't Wanna Say Goodbye pt.1

It came to the time to say goodbye
To the one that I loved and I must leave behind
We made a conclusive decision to go our separate ways
To search for the endeavors that we've tried to find

The kindle of romance had kept our hearts together
But all of our differences had got in the way
By dissuading, to communicate has chosen our fate
Now you've gone away because of the betray of our own dismay

Trying to hold on to a love that was once strong
Dealing with the reality that the desire is gone
Thought by us making love the affection would last long
But deep inside we had known that we were both wrong

I don't want to say goodbye but that is the way it has to be
If only I'd been honest and expressed the true feelings inside of me
Now I fight back the tears that appeared and only my heart can see
Now I'm all alone to face the song of loneliness and grief

Written by
Cheryl Campbell-Divinity

Don't Wanna Say Goodbye-pt.2
Think About Me

Lately, my mind has been racing with vivid thoughts that's escaping
And taking me to moments of rapture but sadly we departed after
Although we went our separate ways, I'm still fascinated of love we displayed
An answer I do seek from questioning, do you still think of me?

The heat rises in the night and excites the desires that you can no long fight
You're not yet set to erect because you want to take your time and please her right
With your motions combined and your bodies intertwined, the passion have inclined
But when she declines your need of ecstasy, sometimes do I come to mind?

I know what we had in the past didn't last, does she compare to me, and I just had to ask
At times, I do reminisce on the precious times spent throughout our relationship
Before our break up, we tried to make up but the feeling didn't take us
Back to when you use to put me in the mood, or the first we made love

We made up our minds and decided to say goodbye and we had to move on
I've been in denial for so long and didn't see the reality of a love that was once strong
Time did healed the pain I concealed but it was revealed while I was all alone
Do you think about us, too, I just wanted to see if you ever thought about me?

Written by
Cheryl Campbell-Divinity

Spread My Wings

Drifting high alone the way
Toward the beams of sunlight
Gliding alone the rugged shores
In the still of the darkest night

Leaping as high as the mountain top
Feeling the wind race against my face
Soaring beyond the open clouds
Swiftly moving into haste

Taking a journey across the sea
While exploring across the ocean ambiance
Watch the sunset by the bay
And the moon shimmering on the ocean front

Venturing across the surfaces of the land
Resting alone the open ground
Being free and much at ease
Contemplating on escaping southern bound

Flying high as a kite
Or as low as the sand
I can spread my wings
And pervade all over the land

Written by
Cheryl Campbell-Divinity

Find a way to escape!

Stones

Most people seem to think that their actions are unseen
They feel the need to judge me and monitor my activities
As I struggled for days to find ways to escape and receive peace
But they still see me as being beneath their level of socialites

You choose to refuse to conclude your own issues that insist to exist
And present resentment of my accomplishment of being content
With stones like boomerangs that ricochet back to your windowpane
I can also claim the same, but I won't gain by exposing you in an open range

You persist on trying to fit and put a bigger dent in my feet print
In that time length, you should have spent to repent and ask for forgiveness
Intense energy flowing immensely from your misery to feed the negativity
An irate altercation can escalate into a case in which I evade a partake

In a house made of glass, your action is cast for each stone that's thrown
Plans he holds for those judgmental individuals who appear to be invincible
What is in the dark will soon part and start to come into clear view
What you decline to realize is that he don't only sees me, he's also watching you

Written by
Cheryl Campbell-Divinity

Those who live in glass a house shouldn't throw STONES!!!

Dedication

Thanks to the Lord for making this possible for me.

This book is dedicated to my brother Frederick Duane Campbell and my Grand Parents, may your souls rest in peace. I will see you all when I get to heaven. To my son, David Hollie Jr. You are going to be a great father. My grandson Jay'den "Nu-Nu" Hollie, my angel. You are the future of greatness. To Karen McCrae, thanks for being a great friend and being there for me .To my mom Lawanna Campbell, where I got my game from, my sister Anissa Campbell, my brother Reggie Campbell, keep being a great author, Linda Bell, you are my auntie, my nieces and nephews and my god daughter Kanisha Graham, you are in my special prayer. Jackie Johnson, you need to hurry up and come down here to have some fun with us. To BJ, you are so crazy. June Haynes, hurry up and make that movie, girl. To Michelle Johnson, you are a great writer, my uncles and my aunt Vickie Gaines in Little Rock and other relatives and friends.

Life is full of choices. Choices to either live your life or just live. Life is a blessing; there are so many obstacles to get through but if you do not take charge, your life is no longer yours.

Whatever choice you make in your life, always put God first.

Divinity

www.ingramcontent.com/pod-product-compliance
Lightning Source LLC
Chambersburg PA
CBHW061512040426
42450CB00008B/1579